THE OTHER HALF OF HISTORY

WOMEN
IN
ANCIENT
GREECE

Fiona Macdonald

PETER BEDRICK BOOKS

NEW YORK

Published in the United States in 1999
by Peter Bedrick Books
A division of NTC/Contemporary
Publishing Group, Inc.
4255 West Touhy Avenue
Lincolnwood (Chicago), Illinois 60646-1975 U.S.A.

Library of Congress Cataloging-in-Publication Data
Macdonald, Fiona.
    Women in ancient Greece / Fiona Macdonald.
      p.   cm.—(Other half of history)
    Includes index.
    Summary: Examines the status and conditions of women in
ancient Greek society, discussing such topics as marriage and family
life, clothing, domestic duties, religion, and more.
      ISBN 0-87226-568-4 (hardcover)
      1. Women—Greece—History Juvenile literature. 2. Women—
Greece—Social conditions Juvenile literature. [1. Women—
Greece—Social conditions—To 146 B.C. 2. Greece—Social
conditions—To 146 B.C.]
    I. Title. II. Series.
    HQ1134.M16 1999   99–21091
    305.4'09495—dc21   CIP

Series editor: Claire Edwards
Series designer: Jamie Asher
Picture researcher: Diana Morris
Consultant: Patsy Vanags

Printed and bound in China
International Standard Book Number: 0-87226-568-4
99 00 01 02 03 10 9 8 7 6 5 4 3 2 1

Picture acknowledgments:

AAA Collection/G.T.Garvey: 34b / © Ronald Sheridan:
front cover c, 3r, 11b, 13b, 15br, 20t, 21, 23t, 23b, 26cr,
31t, 38b, 43tr, 44tr.   Antiken Sammlungen Munchen/AKG London:
42t.   Antiquarian Gallery, NY/Werner Forman:
front cover br, 17bl, 17br.   Archaeological Museum, Dion/
ET Archive: 32bl.   Archaeological Museum, Eleusis/AKG
London/Erich Lessing: 41b.   Archaeological Museum, Naples/ET
Archive: 3cl, 20b.   Ashmolean Museum, Oxford/Bridgeman Art
Library: 7b, 17t, 44bl.

Picture acknowledgments cont:

Bonhams, London UK/Bridgeman Art Library: 33b.   Bridgeman Art
Library: 43br.   The British Museum, by permission of the Trustees:
3l, 9b, 25t, 29t, 40b /AKG London/Erich Lessing: 36b /Bridgeman
Art Library: 4t,18b, 32c /C.M. Dixon:27t /Werner Forman Archive:
3c, 26bl.   Capitoline Museum, Rome/C.M. Dixon: 45c.   James Davis
Photography: 5b.   Fitzwilliam Museum, Cambridge/Bridgeman Art
Library: 15tl.   Werner Forman Archive: back cover t, 6bl,16c.   ©
Sonia Halliday Photographs: 37t.   The Hermitage, St.
Petersburg/Bridgeman Art Library: 6c.   Metropolitan Museum of Art,
Purchase, Walter C. Baker Gift, 1956, (56.11.1) photo © 1992
Metropolitan Museum of Art, NY: 24.   Musée du Louvre/AKG
London/Erich Lessing: front cover bl, 3cr, 9t, 12b, 14l, 18t, 19b, 22b,
28, 29b, 33t, 43tl /Bridgeman Art Library:19t.   Musée Vivenal,
Compiegne/AKG London/Erich Lessing:13t.   Museo Archeologico
Nazionale, Chiusi/AKG London/Erich Lessing:31b.   Museo
Archeologico Nazionale, Napoli/Scala, Firenze: 39t.   Museo
Archeologico, Taranto/Scala, Firenze: 1, 25c.   Museum Narodowe,
Warsaw/AKG London/Erich Lessing: 10b.   National Archaeological
Museum, Athens /AKG London/ Erich Lessing: 8b /C.M. Dixon:7t,
27b, 35 /Werner Forman Archive: back cover b, 16br.   Palazzo
Ducale, Mantua/Bridgeman Art Library:11t. Photostage/© Donald
Cooper: 45t.   © RMN, Paris/H Lewandowski :30b.   Sotheby's New
York/Werner Forman Archive: 39b.   Staatliche Museen,
Berlin/Bridgeman Art Library: 37b.   Villa Giulia, Rome/C.M. Dixon:
41t.   © Wadsworth Atheneum, Hartford/J. Pierpont Morgan
Collection: 34t.

In recent years, a great deal of new material about women in ancient
Greece has been presented. The following, in particular, contain
information not found elsewhere: Sue Blundell, *Women in Ancient
Greece*, British Museum Press, 1997; the authors of conference papers
collected in Sue Blundell and Margaret Williamson (eds), *The Sacred
and the Feminine in Ancient Greece*, Routledge, 1998.

Permissions:

Quotations on pages 6, 8, 12b, 16, 38 and 45 from Josephine
Balmer, *Classical Women Poets* (Bloodaxe Books, 1996).
Quotation on page 9 from Dudley Fitts, *Lysistrata of Aristophanes*
(1962), reprinted by permission of Faber and Faber and Harcourt
Brace & Company.
Quotation on page 28 (73 words) from MENANDER, PLAYS &
FRAGMENTS AND THEOPHRASTUS: THE CHARACTER, by P.
Vellacott, Penguin Books (1967), © P. Vellacott (1967).
Quotation on page 30 from *WOMEN'S WORK: The First 20,000
Years: Women, Cloth, and Society in Early Times* by Elizabeth Wayland
Barber. Copyright © 1994 by Elizabeth Wayland Barber. Reprinted by
permission of W.W. Norton & Company, Inc.
Quotation on page 40 from R. Warner, *Three Greek Plays of Euripides*,
copyright © 1958 by R. Warner. Reprinted by permission of New
American Library Inc., New York.

CONTENTS

The Greek World

The ancient Greek world was made up of the rocky mainland of Greece, together with hundreds of islands, scattered over the Aegean, Adriatic and Ionian seas, and several settlements in countries across the Mediterranean.

A great civilization

The ancient Greeks were proud of their civilization. They felt that they were unique, and that people from other lands were barbarians by comparison. Ancient Greece flourished for more than a thousand years, until the conquering Roman armies arrived. Even after this, Greek civilization did not disappear. Today people still use ancient Greek words, think about ancient Greek ideas and admire their works of art.

Because the Greek civilization was scattered, ships and sailing were important. Myths often described long, dangerous voyages. Here the Greek hero Odysseus is threatened by sirens —creatures that were half-woman, half-bird.

Ancient Greek lands are shaded dark green.

- Massilia

EUROPE

Adriatic Sea

Black Sea

Byzantium

LESBOS

Aegean Sea

ASIA MINOR

Corinth

SICILY • Syracuse

Athens

Sparta

Mediterranean Sea

CRETE

CYPRUS

• Cyrene

Alexandria

AFRICA

ANCIENT GREECE TIME LINE

(c. is short for *circa,* and means "about.")

PREHISTORIC AGE

c. 6000 BC   Farmers settle on the Greek mainland.

BRONZE AGE

c. 3000 BC   The Minoan civilization. Greece is controlled until *c.* 1450 BC by powerful kings based on the island of Crete.

c. 2100 BC   The first Greek-speaking settlers (later known as Mycenaeans) arrive in mainland Greece.

c. 1600–1100 BC   Mycenaean warrior kings rule separate kingdoms in mainland Greece.

IRON AGE

c. 1200 BC   The development of ironworking allows early Greeks to make superior weapons and tools. This helps them take control of Greece.

DARK AGE

c. 1100–800 BC   A time of wars and migration.

c. 800–700 BC   A poet, later known as Homer, composes two poems, the *Iliad* and the *Odyssey*.

ARCHAIC AGE

c. 800–700 BC   Greece is made up of small city-states, each ruled by its own king or noble family.

c. 776 BC   Traditional date of the first Olympic games.

c. 750–600 BC   The Greeks set up colonies in lands around the Mediterranean Sea.

650–500 BC   Tyrants (single strong rulers) and oligarchies (groups of rich men) overthrow the kings and nobles and take control of city-states.

c. 500 BC   Some city-states become democracies.

499–490 BC   The Persians invade Greece.

CLASSICAL AGE

482 BC   Athens leads a group of city-states to fight the Persians.

480–479 BC   The Persians invade again, but are defeated.

460–360   An age of great artistic and scholarly achievements, especially in Athens.

c. 431–404 BC   War between Greek city-states.

404 BC   Sparta defeats Athens and becomes the most powerful city-state on mainland Greece.

336 BC   Greece is invaded, conquered and ruled by Macedonian armies.

HELLENISTIC ERA

336 BC   The Macedonian leader Alexander the Great begins to conquer the empire of Persia.

323 BC   Alexander the Great dies, and his conquests, including Greece, are divided among his generals.

c. 300–200 BC   Greek civilization expands and flourishes in Greek colonies around the shores of the Mediterranean Sea and as far as India.

c. 279 BC   Greece is invaded by Celts.

146 BC   Corinth is destroyed, and soon all of mainland Greece is conquered by the armies of Rome.

The land of Greece was wild, rocky and often infertile. But it was home to a great civilization that lasted thousands of years.

Statues, Temples and Treasures

Wonderful works of art have survived from ancient Greek times. But how much do they tell us about Greek women's lives?

Women shown by men

The ancient Greeks were great artists and craftworkers. Statues, carvings, vase paintings and temples still survive from ancient Greece and are treasured as some of the greatest works of art in the world. They show all kinds of women, from goddesses to housewives. Greek artists, who were mostly men, included women in their work for a number of reasons. They admired female beauty, they wanted to honor the goddesses who protected their cities, or they wanted to create memorials for tombs. Perhaps they wanted to remember their own mothers, daughters and sisters. But in their works, they nearly always showed women differently from men.

Lady Hera, come look down on us,
to your scented shrine
near heaven, look with favour on our
fine-stitched fabric;
with her noble daughter Nossis for
new apprentice
Theophilis wove it, the daughter of Cleocha –
daughter, mother, grandmother, united
in the thread.

VERSE BY NOSSIS, A WOMAN POET WHO LIVED AROUND 300 BC

The silver coin (above) shows the nymph Arethusa, who protected the Greek city of Syracuse, on the island of Sicily in present-day Italy.

This temple at Cape Sounion, near Athens, was built by Greek craftsmen in honor of Poseidon, god of the sea. Men and women worshiped there.

Idealized women

In most Greek art women are hardly ever shown taking action. Instead they stand by, expressing shock or horror, while a male hero fights an enemy or kills a monster. The only women shown carrying weapons or taking part in the action are goddesses. Carvings on tombstones show idealized pictures of women, for example, nursing their children, or putting on beautiful jewels. Wives are also often shown smaller than husbands.

The goddess Athene, protector of Athens, shown in the act of throwing her spear. Active images of women like this one were rare in Greek art.

Women's art

Women produced many beautiful objects themselves, and some even decorated Greek painted pots. But they mainly produced clothes and embroideries, like those mentioned in the poem opposite. They usually worked in materials such as linen, wool and silk, which have long since rotted away. We can read about them in poems and songs, but we will never be able to admire most of them firsthand.

Less visible

The ancient Greeks loved beautiful objects and placed them in their temples, streets, marketplaces and homes. Often these objects were decorated with scenes from everyday life. Statues, carvings, and painted pottery show men farming, fishing, working at various crafts, and going off to war. A smaller number show women. This was because most women did not take part in public life, fight in battles, or have careers. This gave craftsmen a smaller range of topics to chose from.

Although a few women worked in craft studios, most craftworkers were male, and most images of women were made by men.

7

Hidden from History

Compared with some past civilizations, there is very little evidence to tell us about ancient Greece, and little of this evidence is about women. But in recent years historians have found new pieces of information, and have looked again at well-known evidence to discover more about Greek women's lives.

Written by men

Only a limited number of people in ancient Greece could read and write, and nearly all of them were men. We know of only 29 women whose writings have survived, and they were all poets. Where women are mentioned in written documents, such as books on history and science, or records of political speeches, they are seen through the eyes of men. Even legal and government documents are mostly concerned with men, because only men took part in lawmaking and political life.

> On me my Muse has served her summons to sing those beautiful songs of old for Tanagran women in their dawn-white dresses; as the city takes such pleasure in my teasing–trilling songs.
>
> PART OF A POEM BY CORINNA, A WOMAN POET WHO LIVED IN THE GREEK CITY OF TANAGRA, NORTH OF ATHENS, AROUND 300 BC

Although few women could read and write, men often pictured divine women as talented, like the three Muses below. The nine Muses were Greek goddesses. Each one inspired humans in a different area of art or science.

Myths often showed women as dangerous. Here the mythical queen Medea is killing one of her sons to take revenge on her husband.

Women's voices

Although only a few fragments of women's writings have survived, historians think that there may have been a tradition of poems and songs composed by women and passed on by word of mouth from mother to daughter. At times when Greece was ruled by strong city-states, especially during the Classical Age, women's literature was not valued. Later, when Greece was divided into smaller kingdoms, from about 350 BC, women were allowed to play a more active role in art, politics and society, and their writings were appreciated once more.

Women's lives

Even though we rarely know what women thought, we can still discover something about their lives. We know that laws and rules restricted women's legal and personal freedom. Descriptions by men of weddings and religious processions tell us about special days for women and their families. Books by philosophers and scientists, and even myths, tell us what men thought about women and their behavior.

WOMEN BEHAVING BADLY

Give him some actors, a Chorus, an audience, and there he goes proving that women are good-for-nothing ... deceivers, babblers, fly-by-nights, knives in the flesh of honest men.

A SPEECH BY A FEMALE CHARACTER IN A PLAY BY GREEK WRITER ARISTOPHANES, WHO LIVED ABOUT 450–385 BC. HE USES THE CHARACTER TO ATTACK A RIVAL PLAYWRIGHT.

The performance of plays was an important part of Greek city life, especially in Athens in the fifth century BC. Women are often shown as causing death and disaster through their passions, or are bossy, lazy and deceitful. These plays were written as entertainment, but historians think that they reveal men's anxieties about women. Many men thought women were unpredictable and dangerous compared with educated, well-disciplined men. To many Greek men, women were outside normal male society, with its rules and laws. By focusing on women's strange behavior in plays, men strengthened their own ideas of what a well-run community should be.

In ancient Greek drama, all parts were played by men. This clay statue shows a male actor dressed as a woman.

Women's Status

From the earliest years of ancient Greek civilization, women's status was defined by their relationship to men. As Greek society changed, from the age of warrior kings to the age of democracy, women's lives changed too. But men always remained in charge, and women took second place.

> Often I have thought about what it is to be a woman and realized we are nothing. When we are girls our lives are sweet and pleasant at home… But once we grow up, and begin to understand things we have to leave, and become something to be bought and sold…
>
> LINES FROM A PLAY BY THE GREEK WRITER SOPHOCLES, WHO LIVED ABOUT 496–406 BC. ONE OF HIS FEMALE CHARACTERS DESCRIBES WOMEN'S LIVES.

Kings and heroes

Stories composed as long poems by the poet Homer, between about 800 and 700 BC, record a way of life that had existed almost 500 years earlier, when warrior kings ruled Greece. It is dangerous to rely on poetry as a description of real life, but Homer's work, later written down, is our only source for women's lives in that era. One of Homer's woman characters is Penelope, wife of Odysseus. Her usual task is to manage her husband's household, but when Odysseus sets off for war, he leaves her in charge of his lands. Penelope is brave and intelligent, but the poem makes it clear that though she is worthy of respect, she is never equal to her husband.

New laws

By about 500 BC Homer's world of kings and warriors had vanished. Greece was divided into city-states full of soldier-citizens, ruled by tyrants, or oligarchs, or by democracies. City governments made new laws, designed to strengthen the family as the basic unit of society. As a side effect, they controlled women even more than before.

Greek women were expected to support their husbands and sons. This vase painting shows a wife offering wine to the gods before her husband sets off for war.

At the end of the Greek era, goddess worship gave some women more strength as individuals. This carving shows a married couple, with the wife dressed as the Egyptian goddess Isis.

Politics

The city-state of Athens was famous throughout Greece for its democratic system of government. But women had no direct role in political life. They could not attend meetings of the Assembly, where important decisions were discussed and voted on. They could not sit on juries, or serve as government officials. They could not even speak in public, but had to ask their guardian to speak for them. Unlike Homer's Penelope, they could not rule on behalf of absent husbands, or win public respect for their wise acts.

This open space in the city of Athens was called the Pnyx. Male citizens met here to debate government decisions and make new laws.

Classical times

Women remained second-class inhabitants in most city-states until the end of the Classical Age and beyond. Laws varied from place to place, but a woman was usually under the legal control of a man. Her father or closest male relative was her guardian until she married. After marriage her husband, and later her eldest son, took over the task. A woman's guardian had to protect her, provide her with food, clothes and a place to live, and act for her in any dealings with the law. He controlled any goods or property she was given or inherited, and could sell them without her permission. He also had the right to kill any man (except her husband) who had sex with her, and to sell her as a slave to punish her.

11

Love and Marriage

For the ancient Greeks, marriage was an arrangement between families rather than a matter of personal choice for the bride and groom. The richer or more noble a family, the more carefully the arrangement was made. A woman's consent was not required, and she could be married against her wishes.

Marrying a stranger

We have little direct evidence to tell us what ordinary men and women thought of marriage. Poets often wrote about marriage, but their views were contradictory. Love was not normally the main reason for marriage. Some Greek women did not meet their husbands until their wedding day, and there was often a big gap in their ages. Greek girls normally married between the ages of 14 and 18, but most men did not marry until they were about 30 years old.

Before her wedding a bride bathed in water, ideally from a holy spring. Women slaves, or her mother and sisters, perfumed her, helped her dress and made her look her best.

*All those deadly women
Who live with men, and bring them
so much trouble...*

WRITTEN BY HESIOD, A MALE
POET, IN ABOUT 700 BC

*Lucky bridegroom,
the marriage you have prayed
for has come to pass
and the bride you dreamed
of is yours...*

WRITTEN BY SAPPHO, A FEMALE
POET, IN ABOUT 600 BC

Alliances and gifts

Before about 500 BC some noble marriages were arranged between families living in different lands. This was a way of creating political alliances, and was especially important when rival kingdoms were at war. Marriage was also a way of increasing the bride's family's wealth. A bridegroom had to give gifts to the bride's father when a marriage was arranged. A father often interviewed several possible husbands for his daughter, to see who would offer the most.

This painted pot shows a bride preparing for her marriage. Pots like this one were often filled with herbs and placed outside the door of a bride's house on her wedding day as part of the marriage ritual.

Friends and relatives

After about 500 BC marriage customs began to change. Marriages were still arranged between families, and daughters still had no freedom of choice. But most fathers married their children to local families, often to friends and relatives. They wanted the new couple to contribute to their community by creating wealth and providing sons to fight in their city-state army. Daughters were valued as hard-working wives and as future mothers, not for themselves.

Dowries

A groom no longer had to give gifts to the bride's father. Instead fathers gave their daughters money (called a dowry) when they married. This was managed by the bridegroom, and helped support the new family. It also allowed the bride's father to control the groom. If the groom behaved badly, the bride's father could demand that the bride and her dowry be returned. Generous dowries could be used to attract a noble husband, and to increase a father's status in the local community.

Divorce

If a marriage failed, divorce was easily arranged. It could be started by a husband, wife, or wife's family. If a wife left her husband, she normally went back to her family home. In Athens a man had to divorce his wife if she committed adultery, if she turned out to be a foreigner, or if she had no brothers who could inherit her father's land. In that case, when her father died she had to leave her husband and marry a close relative, so that her father's property would not be divided among distant family members.

The bride and groom were driven in a chariot to the groom's family home, where they would live. The vase painting below shows the wedding of a god and goddess, but real brides and grooms traveled in the same way.

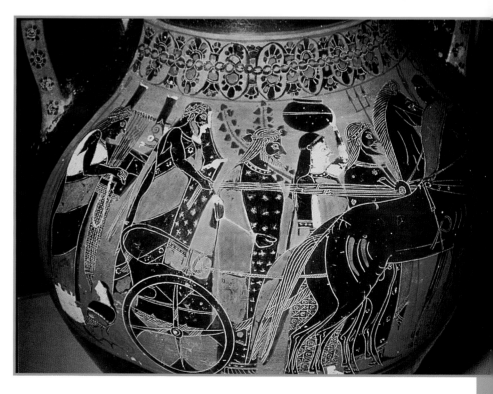

Children

Greek families announced the birth of a new baby to their friends and neighbors by pinning a sign on their front door. For a boy, the sign was a crown of olive leaves (the symbol of victory and success), and for a girl it was a handful of sheep's wool (the symbol of continuous domestic work).

Live or die?

A Greek baby's life depended on its father. If he decided not to keep the baby, it was carried to a public place and left there. It might be picked up by a passer-by and adopted by anyone who needed an extra child, or it might die of hunger. The custom was probably more common at some times than others, such as after a bad harvest. It probably applied mostly to sickly babies. Some historians believe that more girl babies than boys were abandoned in this way.

Not welcome

In most families, daughters were seen as less important than sons and were sometimes given less food. Sons could go out to work. They could defend their homeland, continue a family's name and fame, and run the family business when parents became old. Daughters on the other hand produced little to help the family budget. After about 500 BC they also needed a dowry before they could be married. If they remained unmarried their parents had to support them because respectable women could not go out to work.

Mothers from ordinary families nursed their children themselves. Wealthy women had wet nurses to feed their children for them.

LEAVING CHILDHOOD

Greek girls marked the end of childhood with two special rituals. Once they were old enough to have children, at about 13 years old, they dedicated their childhood toys to the goddess Artemis, then put them away forever. They also began to wear a special decorated belt, or girdle, around their waist, as a sign of their grown-up status. They offered this girdle to the goddess Artemis on their wedding day.

Greek children played with dolls, board games, knucklebones (jacks) and model animals like this clay, pig-shaped rattle.

Growing up

Baby girls and boys were given just one personal name. Girls' names were often female versions of boys' names, such as Hippolyta from the boy's name Hippolytus. Until they were about six or seven, boys and girls played at home, side by side. After this boys were sent to school, where they learned reading, writing, music, math and sports, while girls stayed at home. Boys often stayed in school until they were 18, then joined the army for training for two more years.

Learning at home

Unlike boys, girls met few people from outside their family, and were usually not allowed out alone. Girls stayed at home, where their mothers, or female slaves, taught them spinning, weaving, cooking, child care, and enough writing to help them manage a household. A few girls from wealthy families were taught to read, write and play music by private tutors who came to their homes. But it was difficult for a girl to get a good education, since she was married so young.

This vase painting shows a girl from a rich family reading a papyrus scroll.

BEAUTIFUL BUT DEADLY

Clothes, Hairstyles, Jewelry

Greek men and women both wore tunics, cloaks and sandals. Even so, the customs governing women's clothing meant that women looked very different from men.

Chiton and peplos

The most usual women's garments were long, loose robes with or without sleeves. There were two basic garments, both tunic-shaped. The chiton was the most popular, made of two matching rectangles of cloth, fastened at the shoulders or along the arms by pins or jeweled clips. The peplos, probably an older style, was made of a single length of cloth, wrapped around the body and folded at the top to create a double layer of fabric from shoulder to waist. It was fastened by a big pin on each shoulder and did not have sleeves.

Sometimes stone statues of women, called caryatids, were used to support the roofs of buildings. This one is dressed in a long, sleeveless peplos, fastened at the shoulder with pins.

... my mother [used to say that] in her youth it was thought to be very fine to bind up your hair

with a dark purple [headband] – yes extremely fine indeed, although for a girl whose hair is golden

like a torch-flame [better] to wreathe it in garlands of fresh flowers...

FROM A POEM TO HER DAUGHTER, WRITTEN BY SAPPHO, IN ABOUT 600 BC

This bronze image of the goddess Athene (below) shows her wearing a pleated chiton. Her hair hangs in loose curls. This style was fashionable among young unmarried women in the fifth century BC.

Perfume bottles were made in many shapes and sizes, including this one in the shape of a foot wearing a cork-soled sandal.

Glowing colors

A chiton was usually made of linen and silk, and a peplos of thin woolen cloth. Rich people could afford silk or wool dyed in deep, glowing colors. Both the chiton and peplos were belted at the waist with long, thin strips of fabric, woven with patterns. Underneath, some women wore a piece of cloth wound around the chest, like a bra.

Difficult to move

Long, flowing styles needed no sewing and fitted women of all shapes, and at all stages of pregnancy. But they were not suitable for active work. Men needed to fight on the battlefield or to work on building sites or on farms. So they wore simpler clothes, such as a knee-length chiton, or sometimes just a loincloth or short cloak. Only old men, no longer able to work, wore longer robes.

Cloaks and veils

Outdoors, women covered their clothes with a cloak called a himation. They might shade their heads and even their faces with a kredemnon or veil. Sometimes they also wore a wide-brimmed hat. This was to stop men outside the family from looking at them too closely. It was also fashionable for women to look pale and delicate. Some women covered their faces with white powder. This contained lead and was poisonous, although people did not know it at the time. Some women used makeup to darken their eyebrows and also wore perfume. Both men and women rubbed olive oil into their skin to soften it and to remove dirt.

Hairstyles and jewels

All women, except slaves and those in mourning, wore their hair long. This was a sign of femininity. Men who let their hair grow long were called girlish. Women usually wore their hair tied back in curls and braids, held in place by ribbons or a net. Rich women wore headbands and ornaments made of silver and gold, such as bracelets and earrings. But they did not wear too many jewels or fine clothes outdoors.

This portrait head of a Greek queen shows a fashionable hairstyle in about 220 BC.

Women's Bodies

Greek men admired women for their beauty and charm, and for their housekeeping and motherly skills. But they believed that women were inferior. Their bodies were weaker than men's and unsuited for war. Women's minds were seen as weaker too, so men thought they were less able to think clearly about topics such as politics and philosophy.

Facts and theories

Greek men were the most advanced scientists and doctors in the ancient world. Greek doctors (almost always men, although women could be midwives) prided themselves on their scientific study of disease. They made many important observations, such as that diet, exercise and state of mind can have an important effect on health.

Women were often shown with a mirror (above). But medicine taught that although women seemed beautiful, men's bodies were far superior.

This gold bracelet is decorated with pictures of Artemis, the goddess most closely linked to women's bodies. She protected girls, virgins and mothers in childbirth.

The wandering womb

Greek scientists also held some unscientific theories. Most of these related to women's bodies. Greek doctors thought the womb was a wild thing, able to wander inside a woman's body. If it climbed into the head it caused drowsiness and frothing at the mouth. If it moved toward the chest, the woman might lose her voice. Men saw women as victims of uncontrollable forces inside their bodies. Doctors also believed that women were simply carriers of babies made by men.

The Greeks respected and took care of their bodies. This carving shows Asclepius, the Greek god of healing, and his daughter Hygeia, the goddess of health. She was widely honored in ancient Greek times and her name survives in our word "hygiene."

Double standards

Women had one important function men could not share—the power to give birth to sons who would carry on the man's family name. Because of this, Greek men felt it was important to control women's bodies. Women and girls were carefully supervised. Brides had to be virgins, and wives had to be faithful. In some city-states such as Athens the punishment for a wife sleeping with another man was death. These rules did not apply to husbands, who were free to have affairs as long as they were not with other men's wives.

Sex and pregnancy

Doctors suggested marriage and pregnancy as soon as possible to cure a wandering womb. Marriage was not about love, but about producing children. But pregnancy and childbirth were dangerous times for women and many women died in childbirth, especially young women under 18. The Greek writer Sophocles made one of the female characters in his plays say that she would rather go into battle three times than give birth. He must have heard such comments from women he knew.

Clothes or no clothes

Boys and men often wore few clothes, and played sports and swam naked. Greek artists often portrayed naked men, but women were always shown clothed. Some historians suggest this was because the Greeks saw the male body as normal but the female body as abnormal. Others think that men found veiled women, shut away at home, mysterious and attractive. Either way, women had no choice—men made the rules.

In public, respectable women covered themselves from head to foot to avoid the gaze of strangers.

Wild Women

Many Greek writers and artists thought that women's power to give birth made them closer to nature than men. Greeks saw nature as wild and dangerous. Wolves and bears roamed the countryside, and cities and farms were often shaken by earthquakes. Being close to nature meant that women were wild and dangerous too.

Monsters and plotters

Ancient Greek myths tell of terrifying women monsters, such as the Gorgon, who had snakes for hair and whose poisonous glance turned men and beasts to stone. Plays tell stories of wild women who behaved as good Greek wives should not, by being cunning, or even killing their husbands and children. Greek myths also described women warriors called Amazons, who fought like men. These stories about Amazons were probably based on reports of nomadic tribes who lived in present-day Ukraine.

The artist has given this bronze head of the Gorgon cruel fangs. At first the Gorgon had a lion's face, but over time the Gorgon became a monstrous woman.

An Amazon warrior (on the left) is shown wearing a knee-length tunic over pants and carrying a shield and spear. She is fighting a Greek soldier.

Fear of women

What was the point of these plays and stories, and why did men listen to them? Partly because they were dramatic and exciting. But historians also think that there was another reason. Greek men believed women were different and inferior. They were not truly civilized, they were not educated, they played no part in politics, and they could not be citizens and have civil rights. But they were essential for family life, and for passing wealth from generation to generation. Without them civilization would collapse. The stories about wild women helped men explore their fears. They also gave a reason for men to go on supporting laws and customs that gave them the right to control women's lives.

This painting shows a wild maenad, with loose flowing hair, wearing a panther-skin cloak and carrying a wand. Their wands were said to produce springs of water from the earth and to drip sweet honey. The maenad is whirling around, holding a panther cub by its back leg.

WILD MAENADS

Maenads were groups of women who worshiped Dionysus, the god of wine. Poets and dramatists wrote about how they ran wild in the countryside, dancing and singing, playing with wild animals and tearing goats and cows apart. They also wrote that maenads wore cloaks of animal skins, fastened with snakes, and crowns of snakes and ivy. In real life women did leave their homes to hold religious ceremonies on remote mountainsides in honor of Dionysus. Men saw this as women behaving in their naturally uncivilized state.

... Then, after a nod from their leader, All the maenads whirled their ivy-covered sticks, as a sign that the worship should begin. With one voice they shouted: 'O Iacchus! Son of Zeus! O Bromius!' They went on shouting until all the animals on the mountain seemed wild with holy madness. And when the women ran, all the wild creatures ran with them.

FROM A PLAY BY EURIPIDES, WHO
LIVED ABOUT 485–406 BC

WOMEN AT HOME

Under One Roof

Many Greek households contained three generations: grandparents, a married son and his wife, and their children. The married son's unmarried brothers and sisters might live there too, along with any single female relatives to whom the head of the house was guardian. A man was always head of the household, even if he was not the oldest person living there.

It's no joke, to plunge into a family dinner-party, where First papa leads off the speeches, cup in hand, and gives them all Pointed good advice; mama comes second; then a grandmother Rambles on a little; then great-uncle, in a growling bass; Then comes some old lady who calls you dearest boy. All the time you nod your head and beam at them...

PART OF A POEM BY MENANDER, WHO LIVED ABOUT 340–290 BC

A husband's home

When girls married, they moved to their husband's family home. If their husband's mother was still alive, a bride was expected to obey her. Because women married so young, a wife might become a mother-in-law or even a grandmother before she was 30. Greek grandmothers may also have helped to care for grandchildren, giving them extra love and attention.

Widows

Because of the difference in age between many married couples, a wife was often widowed while she was still young. Widows of childbearing age were likely to marry again. Poor or old widows usually needed family help to survive.

If a widow had sons, she might continue to live with them. If not, she would move back to her parents' home. Wherever she lived, she was not legally independent.

Here a family is shown worshiping together. Worshiping in this way probably strengthened family feeling. Leading worship strengthened a husband's traditional role as head of the household.

Many tombstones show dead women with their families mourning them—death in childbirth was quite common.

Birth and death

A Greek woman might have five or six pregnancies, but probably at least one of her children would die. Possibly 30 percent of babies died in their first year. Other babies were abandoned (see page 14), and there are records of poor women giving up their babies for adoption, because they could not afford to care for them. Many women's lives were marked by times of loss and grief. Poems, plays, tombstones, and temple offerings (asking gods to cure sick children) show that Greek mothers loved their children dearly—perhaps more than they loved their husbands.

This vase shows a slave standing in the hot summer sun holding an umbrella to shade a mother, who watches her son play with a pet bird.

SLAVERY

*I remember the tears pouring down my face
The shattered towers and the walls smashed down
And the oars and spears of our enemies
And ships that carried us so far away
To be sold for gold.*

SPEECH BY A WOMAN SLAVE, CAPTURED IN WAR, FROM A PLAY BY EURIPIDES, WHO LIVED ABOUT 485–406 BC

Greek households included slaves. These were men and women bought from slave traders, sold into slavery as punishment, or captured in war. Some families might own up to ten slaves, but most owned only one or two. Farming families had male slaves to help farm their land, but most household slaves were women, who carried out housework and child care. Slaves had few civil rights. Most slave women could not marry or have children, and could be bought and sold as their owner wished. To most Greeks, a slave was a thing rather than a person.

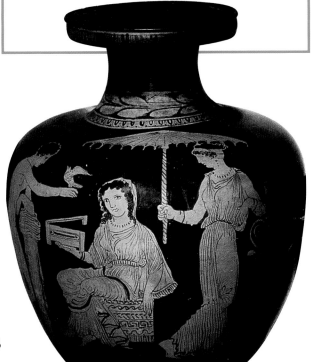

Town and Country Homes

Greek houses were mostly very simple structures, even if they belonged to wealthy families. In towns, houses were usually built of sun-dried mud brick on stone foundations, and had roofs of baked clay tiles. Most homes were single-story, with rooms arranged around a small courtyard open to the sky. There might be a well in the courtyard, and also an oven. Larger homes had two floors, linked by wooden stairs.

Public areas

Greek houses were divided into two separate areas, one for women, called the *gynaikeion*, and one for men, called the *andron*. The men's area contained rooms, including an entrance hall and dining room, where visitors were received and male guests were entertained. In large houses the head of the household also had his own bedroom.

Private rooms

The women's area was often larger. In a wealthy home it might have several rooms on different stories, and include a courtyard where women could enjoy fresh air hidden from public view. The women's area was strictly private. Only family and trusted slaves could enter. Sometimes women visitors might be invited inside, though many husbands disapproved. Women spent their waking hours there, cooking, spinning and weaving, looking after children, and relaxing. Women and children slept there, too, though wives sometimes shared their husband's bed.

This vase painting shows a highly decorated doorway. It has painted columns, probably made of wood, and a checkerboard pattern. The door is strengthened with nails.

Ancient Greek men and women liked to keep clean. Usually women washed in water they or their slaves carried to their homes. This clay model shows a woman sitting in a small, shallow bathtub. Bathers scooped up water from the foot end, which was deeper.

Decorations and furniture

Ancient Greek rooms were simply decorated, with earth, tiles or pebble mosaics on the floor, and a small amount of wooden furniture, such as chests, stools, low tables and beds. The most colorful items were rugs, blankets and wall hangings, woven with complicated patterns by the women themselves. A family might display the best of these on the walls of the dining room, so visitors could admire the unseen women's artistic taste and skill.

Farmhouses

Houses in the country were often larger than homes in crowded towns, since they had extra storerooms, workrooms and barns for animals. They might also have a shaded porch where vines could grow, and where fruits and other wild produce gathered by women, such as herbs and nuts, could be hung up in the sun to dry. Like houses in towns, even the poorest country home would probably have one private room for women's use.

Here a goddess and her worshiper are shown in the goddess's house. There is a beautifully decorated storage chest between them, with a folded robe on it. The footstool, cushioned chair, pottery dishes, bowls and jug are like those from a wealthy Greek home.

WOMEN AND WORK

Running the House

Women from wealthy families spent almost all their time at home, shut away from the outside world, and receiving visits only from family members and female friends. But this did not mean they were idle. Running a household was a full-time job.

Queen bees

One Greek writer described a wife as a queen bee, keeping the workers busy. Servants cooked, cleaned and cared for anyone who was ill. Outdoor workers went on errands to buy food, carry messages, accompany boys to school, or sell household produce. They also brought goods and news into the house from outside. Houses, especially in the country, were built with space to store produce such as grain, oil, wine and fleece. The mistress of the household was responsible for making sure that these were safely stored and managed, so that supplies did not run out before the next harvest.

> *It's not easy for a woman to get out and about. She has to look after her husband, make sure the servant girl does her work, tuck the baby up in bed, wash it, feed it...*
>
> FROM *LYSISTRATA*, A PLAY BY ARISTOPHANES, WHO LIVED ABOUT 450–385 BC

A woman with her maid, who holds the woman's jewelry box. Wives were responsible for training servants and for supervising their day-to-day work.

Wealthy women had some leisure time at home, and knucklebones was a favorite game for women and girls.

Women's work

Indoor workers were mostly women. The Greeks believed that women were softer and more delicate than men, and suited to work in a sheltered environment. Wives were responsible for training other women to do their jobs, and for making sure they performed them well. Their most important work in the home was to make textiles. In cities, most outdoor workers were male.

Power at home

Many married women held a great deal of power. Some husbands gave their wives complete control of the household budget, handing over money for food, fuel and other essentials. Wives were also responsible for guarding the house while their husbands were away from home. In times of war, this might be for months. Many Greek poems and plays refer to wives who question their husbands closely and intelligently about politics, law cases and current affairs, and tell them how they should vote in the law courts or at Assembly meetings. Comic plays show this from a different viewpoint and tell how clever, cunning wives (sometimes helped by female servants) trick their husbands, or manage them skillfully, to get their own way.

Although wealthy women spent their lives indoors, they were not cut off from the outside world. Neighbors visited to share gossip, and older women could give girls advice. Slaves also brought back news from the street and the marketplace.

Hard labor

For poor women, life was quite different. Ordinary women had no slaves or servants to help run the house, but had to do everything themselves. This meant going out to buy food and get water, and working as cooks or cleaners, or helping care for farm animals or weed crops in the fields. Some left the house to work as cooks, nannies, servants, grape pickers, barmaids and garland weavers. In the markets, they also sold many different foods, such as seeds, garlic and vegetables, grown in family gardens, or gathered wild from the hills. They also ran stalls selling fresh-cooked pancakes and bread.

Ordinary women worked hard. Housework was a dirty, tiring, never-ending task. This clay model shows a woman lighting a wood fire.

27

Food and Drink

Greek food was usually simple, but healthy. Ordinary families ate wheat or barley bread, porridge, fruit, olives and vegetables, with a little cheese. In the winter, there were soups made of lentils or dried beans. The Greeks liked the strong flavor of onions, garlic and herbs gathered from mountain slopes. Only wealthy families could afford to eat meat, fresh fish or seafood regularly, or pastries stuffed with honey and nuts. Everyone enjoyed free handouts of meat from animals sacrificed outside temples on religious festival days.

Eating apart

Women mostly did the cooking, which was time-consuming work, with no machines to help them. But men and women did not always eat together. When there were guests from outside the family, women ate in their private area, while men entertained male guests in the dining room. If the family was less wealthy, the men met their guests at the local tavern. If a wife had slaves or servants, she did not serve a meal to her husband's guests herself, but tried to keep herself from view. This was partly because male guests at dinner parties drank so much that they sometimes ended up very drunk and rowdy.

... Now, take those fancy visitors From the islands, reared on fresh-caught fish from far and near – They don't find sea-food all that wonderful; to them It's just a side-dish. Seasoned stuffing, savoury sauce – That's what those gentry go for. Now, an Arcadian – He's different; doesn't live by the sea; what attracts him Is limpets. Then there's your Ionian; rich and coarse. Thick soup I give him ... hot-pots, tasty stews...

PART OF A PLAY BY MENANDER, WHO LIVED ABOUT 340-290 BC

Countrywomen and slaves from city families made their own bread. Poor families bought bread from shops and stalls. This clay model shows a woman from Tanagra, in central Greece, kneading bread dough in a big round bowl.

28

Fresh food

Greece is very hot in the summertime.
Without refrigerators meat, fish, fruits and
vegetables had to be obtained every day.
Since respectable women did not go out
of the house, husbands or slaves went to
the marketplace to buy the freshest food,
and brought it back home. In cities, bread
could be bought at stalls and shops.
In the country housewives made their
own. Country families had plenty of
fruit and vegetables in season,
also milk and cheese. Some
city families kept a goat
in the courtyard to
provide fresh milk.

*Finding fresh water could be a problem in Greece.
Mountain streams were often channeled toward
city centers, so that everyone would have enough
to drink. Here a woman is waiting while her water
jug is filled from a public fountain.*

Water fountains

Water for drinking and washing came from
courtyard wells, or was fetched by poor
women and female slaves from fountains.
These were favorite meeting places, where
women could chat as they waited in line
to fill their water jars. In this way, poor
women were more fortunate than richer
ones—they always had a good reason to
leave the house to get more water, find
a change of scene, and meet their friends.

*This clay model, also from
Tanagra, shows a woman
crouching over a fire,
cooking a meal for
her family. Ordinary
homes had simple
cooking fires like
this, and small
ovens for bread.*

Textile Crafts

Most Greek women, old or young, rich or poor, knew how to spin wool, and to weave it into cloth. After giving birth and caring for children, spinning and weaving were the most essential female tasks.

Home furnishings

Traditionally women made all the bedding, wall hangings, cushions, floor coverings and clothes needed for a household. These items could also be bought at markets. Even noblewomen and queens knew how to spin and weave, but usually they had slaves do the work for them. A skilled slave was very valuable, producing fine goods for her owner, and sometimes extra cloth to sell.

Women wore an epinetron (knee guard) when they prepared wool for spinning. They placed it over their knees to form a steady surface on which to tease out the wool.
This one is decorated with pictures of women preparing and spinning wool.

Wool or flax?

Many families kept sheep, but families with no land could buy raw wool. Wool was the most common fiber used for spinning and weaving, but some women (or their slaves) worked with flax, which was more expensive but produced finer, smoother fabric, suitable for summer clothes. Wool could be dyed brilliant colors. Deep purple, made from a shellfish, was the most expensive. Linen, made from flax, was usually left plain and unbleached, because it did not dye well. The cloth for each garment was woven separately, long lengths for cloaks and women's robes, short for men's tunics.

... is spinning ... with a distaff held in her left hand, twisting the thread, which is weighed down by the spindle.

Making thread

First twigs, burrs and insects were picked from the fleece. Then it was washed, dyed, dried and rolled up. A spinning woman took a roll of fleece and fixed it on a short stick, called a distaff. With her right hand, she twisted a few fibers together, pulling them until they formed a thread. Once this thread was a yard or so long, she wound it around a stick with a weight at one end, called a spindle. She let the spindle drop to the floor. As she twisted more fibers from the fleece the spindle turned, winding the thread onto itself. The thread was then ready to weave.

Weaving cloth

Greek women wove cloth using upright looms. First of all they set up lots of warp threads hanging from the top of the loom, keeping them taut with weights on their ends. Then they carefully took a long weft thread in and out of the warp threads, to produce a length of cloth. The most skillful weavers took months to create wonderful patterns and scenes from legends in their cloth.

FATEFUL WOMEN

The tasks of spinning and weaving were so important in ancient Greece that many myths grew up about them. One of the most famous was about the Fates. The Fates were goddesses who controlled each person's destiny and were shown by artists and writers as three women textile workers:

Klotho *(the spinner)* spun out the thread of life.
Lachesis *(the measurer)* measured out how long a life should be.
Atropos *(the irreversible, no going back)* chose when to cut the thread of life.

This myth links two things about women that the Greeks admired—their ability to create new life and to create cloth.

Women wove cloth on tall upright looms, like the one shown here. The weaver is Penelope, Odysseus's wife (see page 10), with their son.

Entertainers

Respectable women did not join in drinking parties, or appear in public with men who were not related to them, except on religious festival days. Many young men had no women partners, because they did not marry until they were almost middle-aged. For these two reasons, men who wanted to relax in female company often paid women to be with them.

Companions

The best-paid female entertainers were called hetairai, which means companions. They went to parties with men, where they sat beside them, held their hands, amused them with witty conversation, poured wine for them, listened to their worries, boasts and stories, and joined in playing dice or other gambling games. In return for giving a man so much of her time and attention, a hetaira expected to receive expensive gifts. Sometimes she also slept with him, but sex was not always part of the arrangement.

To the flute-girl Bromias ... he gave a silver treasure, and an ivy-wreath of gold... To Pharsalia, a dancing girl ... he gave a laurel crown of gold.

FROM A LIST OF PLUNDERED TREASURES GIVEN BY RULERS FROM THE CITY-STATE OF PHOCIS TO THEIR FAVORITE ENTERTAINERS AND GIRLFRIENDS

At parties people often wore crowns of ivy, in honor of the god Dionysus. Crowns of ivy made in gold were placed in graves to give the dead a happy time in the afterlife.

This cup shows a woman playing kottabos, a popular game played at drinking parties. Players held their drinking cups in one hand and flicked wine toward a target.

This pottery statue shows a woman entertainer strumming a stringed instrument called a cithara.

Beauty and learning

Men admired hetairai for their beauty and gave them luxurious clothes and jewels. A few were also praised for their intelligence and learning. In Athens the hetaira Aspasia was famous for her understanding of politics and philosophy. She was the mistress of Pericles, a leading statesman. Many people believed he discussed political problems with her, and listened to her advice. She was also a friend of the philosopher Socrates, who brought some of his students to talk with her.

This vase painting shows men reclining on couches at a dinner party. They are raising their cups in praise of a female musician.

Dancers and singers

Partygoers were entertained by women musicians, dancers, singers, gymnasts and actors, who performed while the food was served. These entertainers were an essential part of a good evening out. But although they earned more than they could as servants or weavers, they were often seen only as objects, rather than as people with thoughts and feelings. One historian has written that hiring women for a dinner party was as much a part of the preparations as shopping for fish, wine and perfume.

Prostitutes

A third group of women entertainers were even less valued. These were prostitutes, found in almost all Greek cities. They were treated with scorn by their customers, and risked violence and disease. Mostly they were slaves belonging to men who lived off the money they earned, or very poor women who had no other way of paying for food and shelter. Some may have started life as babies abandoned because they were female.

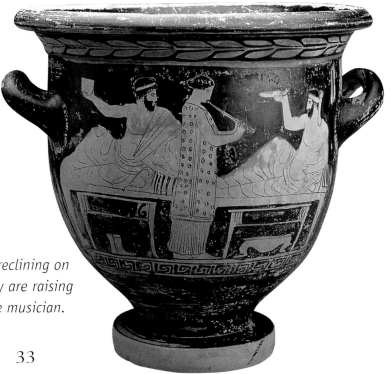

WOMEN IN SPARTA

An Unusual Society

Women's lives were similar in many parts of ancient Greece, but the Greeks themselves singled out the city-state of Sparta, in southern Greece, as being very different. In particular Athenian men (our main source of evidence) commented on the lives of Spartan women, noting their freedom and their lack of modesty.

State not family
Individual families headed by a husband were not important in Sparta. Instead, the state laid down rules for everyone. Boys were sent away from home at the age of seven to train as soldiers. They lived in army barracks until they were 30. Even after that, men might be absent for months, fighting in wars. This meant that Spartan women had to be independent. They had to manage households all alone. Unlike other Greek women, Spartan women could own land and property and decide how it should be run.

The men of Sparta always did what their wives told them, and let women take part in public affairs, even though men were not allowed to share in household organization.

COMMENT BY THE ROMAN AUTHOR PLUTARCH, WHO LIVED ABOUT AD 0–120

Spartan warriors were feared throughout Greece for their bravery and discipline. This bronze statue shows a Spartan soldier dressed in a plumed helmet, ready for war. Unlike other Greek men, Spartan warriors wore their hair long and flowing.

Sparta was cut off from the rest of Greece by high mountains and wild countryside and developed its own ideas about society and government.

Free and easy

Spartan women also took part in public life, freely expressing their views on current affairs. The government believed that an indoor life was unhealthy, and encouraged women and girls to take part in outdoor sports. Even pregnant women were urged to exercise, to help them give birth to stronger babies. Spartan girls (like men and boys in other parts of Greece) played sports with few clothes on. Sportswomen wore short tunics, slit high at the thigh, to allow for plenty of movement.

Spartan weddings

Spartan marriage customs were unlike any others in Greece. On her wedding day, a bride cut her hair short, dressed in men's clothes, and met her husband after dark in a secret hideaway. He then went back to his army barracks and only spent occasional nights with her until he retired from full-time war service at the age of 30. Women married late by Greek standards, when they were 18 or over, to men aged about 25. This closeness in age, compared with couples in Athens for instance, may have helped wives feel more equal with their husbands.

This statue shows a Spartan girl athlete. She looks strong and healthy, and is wearing clothes that would have been shocking in other parts of Greece.

Shocking behavior

Spartan behavior after marriage was also commented on and criticized by other Greeks. Wives could be married to more than one man at a time, usually to their husband's brothers. Men who had no children might ask husbands if they could borrow their wives to produce heirs. We do not know what Spartan women thought of these arrangements, but it is possible that they had to give permission, since they had rights unknown to women anywhere else in Greece. For example, they could choose men as lovers while their husbands were away, and bring up children from such affairs as part of the family. Such freedom may have begun as part of a government scheme to breed lots of new citizens, to make Sparta a powerful city-state.

Priestesses

The ancient Greeks believed there were many gods and goddesses, and most of these had their own temples, looked after by priests and priestesses. Both priests and priestesses supervised worship and offered prayers and sacrifices to the gods. Sometimes they also sang and danced.

Servants of the gods

As a duty, some ancient Greeks spent time as priestesses or priests, but it was not a full-time occupation. Women served goddesses and men served gods, though there were exceptions to this rule. Animal sacrifices were normally carried out by male temple staff, while women usually wove clothes for a holy statue or cleaned the temple treasures. In many ceremonies priests and priestesses had to carry out a set number of rituals in the correct order, otherwise the gods' power might be weakened. This holy knowledge was passed down through their families.

And there, too, is something wonderful, whose fame will last for ever, Young women from Delos, who serve Apollo, god of hunting, First they sing in praise to Apollo, Then they praise Leto, his mother, and his sister, death-dealing Artemis...

DESCRIPTION OF WOMEN SINGERS IN APOLLO'S TEMPLE AT DELOS, FROM A POEM PROBABLY WRITTEN AROUND 700 BC

Priestesses prepare two bulls for sacrifice to the gods. They have washed the animals and are tying flowers around their necks. They will lead them to the altars outside the temple, where priests will kill them.

The Greeks believed they could feel especially close to gods at certain places. This is the site of the temple of the god Apollo at Delphi.

Acting out myths

Some rituals reenacted stories about past miracles. Priests and priestesses often played a leading part in these holy dramas, and acted the parts of goddesses and gods. Each year the wife of one of the chief magistrates of Athens became a priestess for the year that her husband held this position. She made secret offerings to the god Dionysus on behalf of the city, and took part in a ceremony where she was married to the god.

Public office

Being a priestess was the only public office a woman could hold. In Athens, the city-state we know most about, there were more than 40 priestesses employed at major shrines. Priestesses at the most important shrines, such as the temple of Athene, the goddess who protected the city, often came from the most noble families. The senior priestess of Athene was respected almost as if she were a man. Sometimes her religious actions were interpreted as signs of good or bad luck and helped shape government plans.

The Greeks believed that the gods sent them messages in different ways—in dreams, through natural events such as lightning, or through oracles. An oracle was usually a priest or priestess who claimed to be able to tell the future by communicating with the gods. The most famous oracle was the Pythia, a priestess at the temple of Apollo in Delphi, near Athens. People believed that Apollo took possession of the Pythia while she was in a trance. She then spoke with his words, and could be asked for advice. At first the Pythia was always a young virgin. Later she was usually a woman over 50 dressed as a girl. She could be married, but had to live apart from her family. No one knows how Pythia priestesses were chosen, but they seem mostly to have been ordinary women. Sometimes there were several at a time, working in shifts. Most historians think the answers they gave were provided by male advisers.

A king is consulting the Pythia oracle at Delphi. She is shown holding a spray of leaves, which were burned to create overpowering fumes.

Women Worshipers

One Greek male writer stated: "It is more appropriate for a woman to remain at home and not be out of doors." He was putting forward the usual view of how women should spend their lives. But there was one important exception to this rule. Women were expected to leave home to share in religious ceremonies of many different kinds. For the Greeks, religious rituals were an important way of keeping the goodwill of the gods and of strengthening the community.

Processions and games

The Greeks felt that the gods played an active, important part in their lives. Most acts of worship were thanksgiving for past kindnesses from goddesses or gods, or offerings designed to ask them for protection or for favors. Each city had its own favorite god or goddess, and honored them with processions, music, dancing and even sports competitions. The Olympic Games began in this way, in praise of Zeus, king of the gods. They were for men only, but there were also female games, in honor of the goddess Hera, Zeus's wife.

> We've come to worship mother Demeter –
> a circle of nine,
> all girls of a certain age, all dressed
> up in our holiday best –
> dressed in our best, and wearing our
> finest ivory jewels
> stars sawn from the shining sky,
> a sight that should be seen.
>
> PROBABLY WRITTEN BY THE WOMAN POET
> ERINNA, WHO LIVED AROUND 350 BC

This temple at Olympia was built in about 600 BC and dedicated to the goddess Hera. The ruins still stand in modern Greece.

This ... shows women offering wine to an image of Dionysus, god of wine and drama. The image is made of a wooden pole, clothes and a mask. Myths told how Dionysus had special powers over women to make them run wild.

Women's festivals

Some religious festivals were celebrated only by women. The most famous of these was the Thesmophoria, celebrated in Athens for three days in autumn. On the first day, women left their homes and families and met at the Pnyx, the hill where men held political debates. The next day, they sat all day on the ground in the open air, and ate no food. They spent the evening shouting out insults and rude words. On the final day they held a big feast and made offerings to Demeter of rotting piglets and cakes, which they had buried several months before. These offerings were later scattered on fields, to encourage the crops to grow. Historians have suggested different meanings for such festival events. They may have been a fertility ritual, celebrating women's ability to have children, or a thanksgiving for women's contribution to civilized life. According to myth, it was only after the goddess Demeter taught the earliest Greek people to plant seeds and harvest grain that Greek civilization really began.

Private worship

Processions and festivals were for special days. They took place on set dates in a city's religious calendar. Individual families also arranged their own ceremonies in public temples at important moments, such as on the birth of a child. For everyday worship each house had an altar, where the family made offerings to the gods. Men usually led these rituals, but women made offerings and said prayers of their own, especially to Hestia, guardian of the household, and Artemis, goddess of childbirth.

Long-eared wheat was an early form of wheat grown in Greece. Women offered stalks of wheat to the goddess Demeter on family altars. This is an offering of wheat made of gold.

Death and the Afterlife

There is no clear description of Greek funeral customs, but historians have pieced together what may have taken place, from evidence such as pottery, law codes and plays. Men and women had different roles to play at funerals. From this we can see how important women were in a family's private life. Women helped a family cope with its religious and emotional needs, as well as performing funeral customs in the proper way.

Flowers and herbs

When a person died their body was carried home, if it was not already there. Women from the dead person's family then washed the body, wrapped it in cloth and decorated it with flowers and herbs. The body was placed on a wooden board in the dining room, the main room of a house, with its feet facing the door. Unmarried teenage girls might be dressed in wedding robes. Rich people might wear jewelry.

Mothers have lost their children, maidens have cut from their heads their tresses [long hair] in mourning for their brothers... Hands are laid to the head; fingernails tear the delicate skin of the cheek which is wet from the flowing of blood.

DESCRIPTION OF WOMEN MOURNERS, FROM A PLAY BY EURIPIDES, WHO LIVED ABOUT 485–406 BC

Women mourners usually followed a corpse to the burial ground. You can just see the dead person's head, with its wreath of leaves. The women have cut their hair as a sign of respect. Some are also wearing black robes. The songs they sang as sad laments were passed down through the centuries.

This girl is making offerings at an altar. By performing funeral ceremonies correctly and behaving with respect toward the dead, women won honor for the family.

Mourners

A jar of oil was placed close to the body and a pot of water was put next to the front door of the house to protect people from spiritual pollution. The next day, friends and family came to mourn. Women stood close to the body, wept loudly, waved their arms, and even cut their hair or scratched their faces. Men simply raised their hands in a sign of respect and greeting. If they made any noise, it was probably a formal prayer or song. Only old men were allowed to weep like women.

To the cemetery

Three days after death, the body was carried out of the house before dawn for burial. Men led the way to the cemetery. Women followed, weeping and wailing. Sometimes paid musicians and mourners took part in the procession. These were usually women. Men arranged the digging of the grave, and sacrifices of animals, food and flowers. After the sacrifices, everyone returned to the dead person's family home for a funeral meal prepared by the women.

Guardians of family history

Mourning continued for another 30 days, after which the Greeks believed the soul was free to leave the body. The dead person's home was ceremonially swept clean, and the sweepings were placed on the tomb. Like funeral processions, cemetery visits were times when even the most shut-away women were allowed to appear in public. Some historians have also suggested that through funeral rites such as these, women may have acted as guardians of unwritten family histories. As they prepared the body and welcomed friends they may have passed on memories of the dead person, and of other family members who died long ago.

In Greek myth, Hecate (seated) was queen of the Underworld. The Greeks believed that dead people's spirits were carried there and survived as shadows as long as people remembered them.

Goddesses

The ancient Greeks honored local gods and spirits, as well as heroes and heroines—ordinary humans who had done great deeds and become almost godlike. But they believed that the most important gods lived on Mount Olympus. There were six gods and six goddesses in the main Olympian family. Both men and women prayed to them, but there were special women-only festivals, in honor of goddesses, and ceremonies marking different stages in women's lives. The most important goddesses had powers to protect virgins, homes, unhappy wives, bereaved parents or women in childbirth.

Hera is wrapped in a cloak and carries a scepter, as a sign of royal power.

Hera

Hera was the goddess of weddings and marriage and the guardian of faithful wives. A special women-only sports festival was held at Olympia every four years in her honor. In myths she is shown as a majestic queen, yet also as the jealous wife of Zeus, king of the gods, who chased after countless other women.

Athene

Athene was the wise guardian goddess of the city of Athens. She rejected the female roles of wife and mother, but was patron of crafts, including spinning and weaving. She was born fully armed from the head of her father Zeus, and was a mighty warrior, helping her favorite male heroes. Unlike mortal wives and daughters, she did not have to be guarded and controlled, and did not show obedience to men, except to Zeus.

Artemis

Artemis was the goddess of hunting and the countryside, and protector of unmarried girls. She was the daughter of Zeus, and twin sister of Apollo, the sun god. Artemis was helpful to women at three stages in their lives: reaching adulthood, getting married, and childbirth. She was associated with life-giving blood, fertility and violent death. Like Athene, she remained powerful and independent of men.

Aphrodite, goddess of love, carved by a famous sculptor called Praxiteles, who lived in about 400 BC.

Hestia has been carved here as a young Greek housewife.

Aphrodite

Aphrodite was the goddess of love. A few poems, some by women, praise her sweetness and charm, but more myths tell of the harm she created by causing gods and mortals to fall in love. She was not a good mother. For the Greeks, love, wifely virtues and motherhood did not mix. Some historians think that a goddess who combined all of these would have given too powerful an image of women.

Demeter

As fertility goddess, Demeter protected crops. She was also the only Greek goddess who gave a positive view of motherhood. A famous myth told how Persephone, her daughter, was kidnapped by Hades, god of the Underworld. Demeter vowed that no crops would grow until she found her child. She rescued Persephone from the Underworld but, because Persephone had eaten food there, had to let her go back for one third of each year. This myth clearly reflects the process in which crops die each autumn but grow again in spring.

Demeter (center) on her way to the Underworld to find her daughter Persephone.

Hestia

Hestia was the goddess of the hearth, which was the most important part of any house, and a symbol of a wife's rightful place. Brides were led to the hearth as soon as they arrived in their new family's home, and women made offerings of food there to Hestia every day. Newborn babies were carried around the hearth as a sign that they were accepted into the family. Hestia represented warmth and safety.

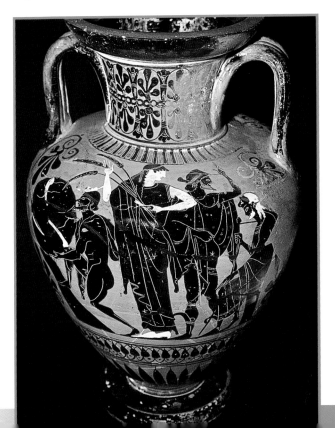

Famous Women

Only a few names of real Greek women have come down to us. Women could not lead public lives or gain the skills necessary to become famous. The most familiar women appear in Greek myths, where they are often shown as brave and independent, whether for good or evil. Although myths do not give an accurate view of real life, and are exaggerated to make a better story, they do show us images of women familiar to men and women throughout the Greek world.

Pandora

According to myth Pandora was the first woman, created by the god Zeus as a deadly gift to punish men for playing a trick on him. All the gods helped to equip Pandora for life as a woman, giving her jewels, beauty and charm, but also cunning and the ability to inspire love. Zeus then gave her a jar, which he ordered her never to open, and sent her into the world as a trap for men. Being a woman and therefore curious (the Greeks said), she opened the jar and all the evils in the world poured out. Only hope was left inside. Pandora's story carried a message about women: men couldn't live without them, but they would bring terrible trouble.

Helen (right) is led back to her husband, King Menelaus, and her home in Greece.

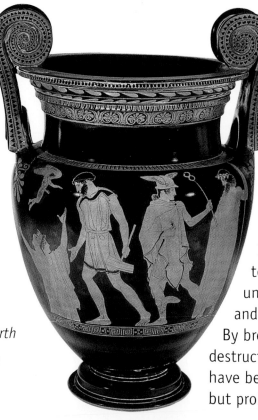

This Greek artist has shown Pandora still emerging from the earth she was created from.

Helen of Troy

In Greek poetry Helen was the beautiful wife of King Menelaus of Sparta. Helen was captured by Paris, son of King Priam of Troy (in Turkey). In some versions she left her husband and children to run away with Paris. The Greeks went to war against the Trojans to capture Helen and bring her home. Everyone blamed Helen for the war. If she had not allowed her beauty to be seen, or if she had not been unfaithful to her husband, Greece and Troy could have lived in peace. By breaking the rules Helen brought destruction and death. In reality, there may have been a war between Troy and Greece, but probably over farmland and crops.

Plays by ancient Greek writers about honorable and brave women are still performed today. Above, Antigone is shown surrounded by a Greek chorus in an adaptation of Sophocles' play.

There are no real-life portraits of Sappho. This one (right) was carved after her death. It doesn't show us what she looked like, but it tells us how much she was admired. Only respected people were honored with statues.

Sappho

Sappho is one of the few real women from ancient Greece whose fame has survived. She was a poet who, unusually for her time, wrote about women's thoughts and feelings. In one poem she wrote, "Love shook my heart like the wind on the mountain rushing over the oak trees." She also experimented with language to create dramatic pictures. She was praised during her lifetime and inspired some of the best male writers in Greece and Rome. We know little about Sappho's life. She was born about 600 BC on the Greek island of Lesbos and probably came from a wealthy family. She may have taught poetry to girls, or she may have written alone, for herself, her family and friends.

Antigone

In about 440 BC the playwright Sophocles wrote a play called *Antigone*. It retold an ancient myth in order to make his audience in Athens think about issues of right and wrong. It also showed how a woman could uphold the highest standards of Greek behavior. The play's heroine Antigone is a Greek princess. King Creon, the local ruler, gives orders that her brother, killed as a traitor, should not be buried but left for wild animals to devour. This risks breaking the gods' holy laws, but Creon threatens to kill anyone who disobeys him. Antigone decides to obey the gods and bury her brother. She then kills herself before the king's men can execute her. Creon realizes that he has been wrong and sends an order to pardon her, but it is too late.

Aspasia

Aspasia was a hetaira who lived in Athens during the fifth century BC. She entertained many of the city's artists, thinkers and writers at her home, and took part as an equal in their discussions. In about 435 BC Pericles, one of the greatest political leaders of Athens, fell in love with her. He divorced his wife and invited Aspasia to live with him. She was said to have helped him prepare many of his speeches. Pericles' opponents attacked her, saying that she was immoral, an atheist, a foreigner (not an Athenian) and possibly a spy. Pericles made a powerful speech to defend her and was supported by his fellow citizens. Aspasia and Pericles lived together until he died of a plague which swept through Athens in 429 BC.

GLOSSARY

adultery Having sex with someone else's husband or wife.

Alexander the Great A king of Macedonia who conquered a vast empire from about 330 BC, stretching from Greece to India.

alliance An agreement between people or nations.

army barracks Buildings where soldiers live.

Assembly The main decision-making body in Athens. It met every day to discuss government plans, and appointed officials to run the city.

atheist Someone who does not believe in God.

barbarians The Greek word for foreigners. The Greeks said foreign speech sounded like "bar bar bar."

ceremony A gathering of people, with processions and prayers, held in honor of a special event.

chorus In Greek drama the chorus is a group of actors who comment on the main action of the play.

citizen A person who lives in a city or country and has rights as a member of the community there. Only men could be citizens in ancient Greece. Women were only daughters and wives of citizens.

city-state A city and the surrounding countryside, farms and villages, with its own laws and government.

civil rights The rights that allow an ordinary person to play a full part in society, such as having a say in which laws are passed and how the government is run.

colony A community of settlers who keep in contact with their homeland.

civilization A society with its own laws, customs, beliefs and artistic traditions.

current affairs The term for describing business, politics, wars and lifestyles.

customs The established way of doing things.

debate Public discussion between people who hold different views from one another.

democracy A system of government that allows its citizens to share in making decisions about how their country should be run.

divine Belonging to the gods.

dowry Money and property brought by a bride to a marriage.

fertility ritual Ceremonies designed to help people produce babies, or land to grow crops.

guardian A person who is legally responsible for looking after someone else.

hearth The fireplace, sometimes also used for cooking, at the center of a home.

hetaira A female entertainer and paid companion to men. The plural is hetairai.

holy spring A spring associated with a god or goddess, believed to have special powers.

immoral Breaking society's laws of behavior.

inherit To pass on goods or land from one generation to another.

idealized More perfect than reality.

juror A member of the public who sits in a law court to decide whether someone is guilty of a crime. A group of jurors make up a jury.

knucklebones Tiny anklebones from sheep and goats used to play a game, in which the bones are thrown in the air and picked up again.

law code The laws that govern a country or city.

legally independent Treated as an independent person by the law, able to express opinions, own property, and live on one's own.

magistrate A senior law officer.

memorial A work of art made to help people remember someone who has died.

midwife A woman trained to help mothers in childbirth.

mosaic A picture made of little pieces of colored stone or glass carefully fitted together.

mourner Someone who shows sorrow at a funeral.

Muse One of nine Greek goddesses who inspired science, music, drama and the arts.

myth A story that communicates important beliefs about people and how they live. Ancient Greek myths were mainly stories about gods, goddesses, heroes and heroines.

nymph A spirit of nature, for instance of a tree or river, who appears as a young woman.

lfferings Gifts offered to the gods and goddesses.

oligarchs Groups of rich male rulers.

papyrus An early form of paper made from reeds.

philosopher Someone who studies how to find knowledge, wisdom and truth.

public life Taking part in the world outside the home, such as government and law. Public office is a job in the government or army or navy.

ritual The set form of a ceremony.

sacrifice Killing an animal to please the gods.

shifts Periods of work.

shrine A holy place. Also the holiest part of a temple, where the statue of a god or goddess is kept.

statesman A well-respected politician.

trance A dreamlike state of mind.

tyrant A powerful ruler who governs without paying any attention to existing laws or customs.

Underworld The place where the Greeks believed dead people's spirits went after death.

warp and weft Warp threads hang vertically, while weft threads are woven horizontally through them.

Further reading
What Life Was Like at the Dawn of Democracy: Classical Athens, 525–322 B.C. Time-Life Books, 1997.

How We Know About the Greeks. John and Louise James. Peter Bedrick Books, 1998.

Ancient Greece: Daily Life. Stewart Ross. Peter Bedrick Books, 1999.

Myths and Civilization of the Ancient Greeks. Hazel Mary Martell. Peter Bedrick Books, 1998.

The Atlas of the Classical World. Piero Bardi. Peter Bedrick Books, 1997.

For older readers
Goddesses, Whores, Wives and Slaves: Women in Classical Antiquity. Sarah B. Pomeroy. Schocken Books, 1995.

Women's Work: The First 20,000 Years. Elizabeth Wayland Barber. W.W. Norton & Co., 1994.

Gods, Men and Monsters from the Greek Myths. Michael Gibson. Peter Bedrick Books, 1977.

INDEX